Connect the dots from 2 to 30. Count by 2s. Start at the ★. Color the pict

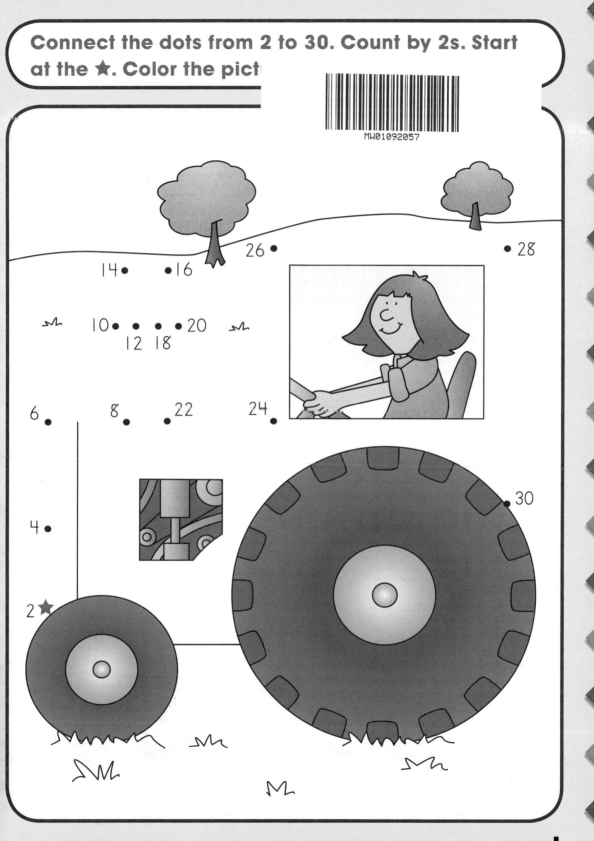

14• •16

26•

• 28

10• • • •20
12 18

6• 8• •22 24•

•30

4•

2★

MW01092057

Solve each problem. Use the key to color each balloon. Then, circle the balloon with the smallest sum.

2 = red   4 = yellow   6 = blue   7 = orange
8 = green   10 = purple

$$\begin{array}{r} 3 \\ + 3 \\ \hline \end{array}$$

$$\begin{array}{r} 4 \\ + 6 \\ \hline \end{array}$$

$$\begin{array}{r} 5 \\ + 2 \\ \hline \end{array}$$

$$\begin{array}{r} 2 \\ + 2 \\ \hline \end{array}$$

$$\begin{array}{r} 5 \\ + 3 \\ \hline \end{array}$$

$$\begin{array}{r} 4 \\ + 2 \\ \hline \end{array}$$

$$\begin{array}{r} 2 \\ + 0 \\ \hline \end{array}$$

$$\begin{array}{r} 4 \\ + 4 \\ \hline \end{array}$$

Solve each problem. Match the answers to the numbers below. Write the correct letters on the lines.

7 − 2 B	5 − 4 A	9 − 3 R	14 − 8 F
15 − 9 C	12 − 6 D	5 − 5 L	10 − 8 E
16 − 8 U	9 − 2 T	6 − 3 J	18 − 9 W
7 − 3 P	11 − 8 Q	12 − 1 H	13 − 3 Y

What is the largest animal in the ocean?

___ ___ ___ ___ ___ ___ ___
7   11   2   5   0   8   2

___ ___ ___ ___ ___
9   11   1   0   2

CD-104367

3

Use the graph to answer each question. Write each number as a number word. Then, write the first letter of each answer in order on the lines.

Animals at the Aquarium

Number

Type	1	2	3	4	5	6	7
shark	■						
clam	■	■	■				
fish	■	■	■	■	■	■	■
starfish	■	■	■	■	■		
octopus	■	■	■	■			

1. Are there more fish or clams? _____

2. How many sharks are there? _____

3. Are there more octopuses or sharks? _____

4. How many animals are there in all? _____

What does a clam have that the other animals at the aquarium do not? A _____ _____ _____ _____

Solve each word problem. Match the answers to the numbers below. Write the correct letters on the lines.

1. There were 8 sharks swimming around a coral reef. Soon, 5 more sharks joined them. How many sharks were there in all?

O

2. A school of 10 fish was swimming under a boat. Then, 3 fish swam away. How many fish were left?

L

3. Desiree saw 9 dolphins diving in the ocean. Then, 3 dolphins jumped. How many dolphins did not jump?

H

4. On a scuba diving trip, Trina saw 7 sea horses, 3 clams, and 1 octopus. How many animals did she see altogether?

S

5. Morton found 10 crabs in a tide pool. Two were red. How many were not red?

C

6. There were 7 hatched sea turtles in the nest. Then, 10 more sea turtles hatched. How many sea turtles hatched in all?

O

Where do fish learn to swim?

In a ____ ____ ____ ____ ____ ____
       11   8   6   17   13   7

Solve each problem. Color a banana in each bunch when you find a matching sum. Circle the bunch with the most bananas colored.

47   68   97   39   76   54

32	52	84	19	61
+ 15	+ 16	+ 13	+ 20	+ 15

44	31	23	32	45
+ 10	+ 23	+ 24	+ 36	+ 52

61	35	63	24
+ 36	+ 12	+ 13	+ 15

36	41	82	34
+ 40	+ 13	+ 15	+ 34

CD-104367

6	8	3	4
+3	+1	+3	+5

6	1	4	3	0
+0	+1	+4	+4	+7

7	4	2	6	5
+1	+2	+2	+2	+1

- - - - - - - - - - - - - -

6	8	3	4
+3	+1	+3	+5

6	1	4	3	0
+0	+1	+4	+4	+7

7	4	2	6	5
+1	+2	+2	+2	+1

 CD-104367

5	6	5	1	5
− 2	− 0	− 3	− 1	− 4

3	9	9	4	6
− 2	− 3	− 7	− 1	− 2

7	8	8	9	
− 5	− 2	− 3	− 4	

- -

5	6	5	1	5
− 2	− 0	− 3	− 1	− 4

3	9	9	4	6
− 2	− 3	− 7	− 1	− 2

7	8	8	9	
− 5	− 2	− 3	− 4	

How many problems can you solve in one minute?

STARTING LINE

$$\begin{array}{r} 9 \\ -1 \\ \hline \end{array} \qquad \begin{array}{r} 8 \\ -5 \\ \hline \end{array} \qquad \begin{array}{r} 6 \\ -4 \\ \hline \end{array}$$

$$\begin{array}{r} 6 \\ -1 \\ \hline \end{array} \qquad \begin{array}{r} 9 \\ -2 \\ \hline \end{array} \qquad \begin{array}{r} 8 \\ -3 \\ \hline \end{array} \qquad \begin{array}{r} 8 \\ -8 \\ \hline \end{array} \qquad \begin{array}{r} 6 \\ -2 \\ \hline \end{array}$$

$$\begin{array}{r} 7 \\ -4 \\ \hline \end{array} \qquad \begin{array}{r} 8 \\ -2 \\ \hline \end{array} \qquad \begin{array}{r} 9 \\ -7 \\ \hline \end{array} \qquad \begin{array}{r} 8 \\ -6 \\ \hline \end{array} \qquad \begin{array}{r} 6 \\ -3 \\ \hline \end{array}$$

FINISH LINE

$$\begin{array}{r} 5 \\ -2 \\ \hline \end{array} \qquad \begin{array}{r} 5 \\ -4 \\ \hline \end{array} \qquad \begin{array}{r} 7 \\ -2 \\ \hline \end{array} \qquad \begin{array}{r} 7 \\ -5 \\ \hline \end{array}$$

Answers Correct: _____

Determine the place value of each underlined digit. Then, use the key to color each car.

ones = red   tens = blue   hundreds = green

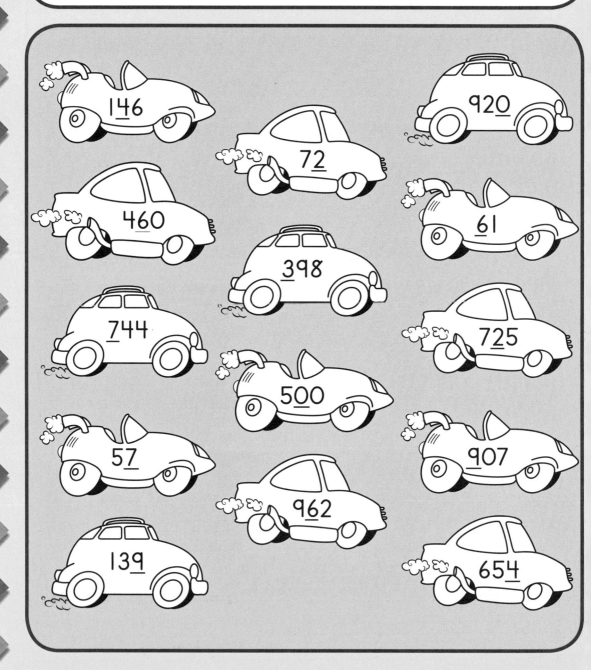

CD-104367

© Carson-Dellosa

Circle the problems hidden in the puzzle. Problems can be found across and down. Write – and = between the numbers to complete each problem.

$18 - 9 = \underline{\ 9\ }$ $11 - 5 = \underline{\quad}$ $13 - 5 = \underline{\quad}$

$15 - 7 = \underline{\quad}$ $17 - 9 = \underline{\quad}$ $12 - 6 = \underline{\quad}$

$17 - 8 = \underline{\quad}$ $15 - 8 = \underline{\quad}$ $14 - 5 = \underline{\quad}$

$14 - 7 = \underline{\quad}$ $14 - 6 = \underline{\quad}$ $13 - 4 = \underline{\quad}$

$13 - 6 = \underline{\quad}$ $11 - 6 = \underline{\quad}$ $14 - 8 = \underline{\quad}$

$12 - 5 = \underline{\quad}$ $16 - 9 = \underline{\quad}$ $12 - 4 = \underline{\quad}$

11	6	5	15	3	12	11	14
14	16	14	7	7	5	5	8
5	7	15	8	7	7	6	6
9	9	11	14	13	4	9	12
18	4	13	6	7	17	9	6
9	13	5	8	17	9	9	6
9	1	0	2	8	8	4	7
12	4	8	8	9	16	9	7

Write the missing numbers to complete each number pattern.

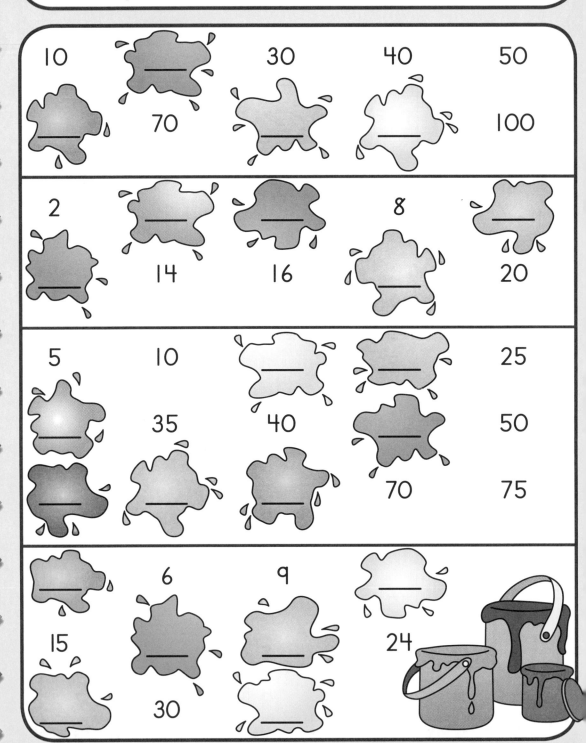

Row 1: 10, ___, 30, 40, 50, ___, 70, ___, ___, 100

Row 2: 2, ___, ___, 8, ___, 14, 16, ___, 20

Row 3: 5, 10, ___, ___, 25, 35, 40, ___, 50, ___, ___, ___, 70, 75

Row 4: ___, 6, 9, ___, 15, ___, ___, 24, 30

CD-104367

Draw the hands on each clock. To solve the riddle, write the letters from the clocks with times half past the hour in order. Then, write the letters from the clocks with times on the hour in order.

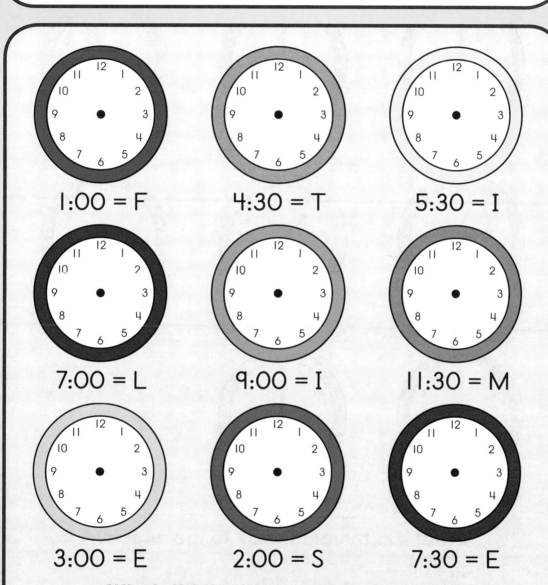

1:00 = F

4:30 = T

5:30 = I

7:00 = L

9:00 = I

11:30 = M

3:00 = E

2:00 = S

7:30 = E

What did the bird say when he saw another bird wearing a watch?

" ____ ____ ____ ____ ____ ____ ____ "

Under each clock, write the time shown. Match the answers to the times below. Write the correct letters on the lines.

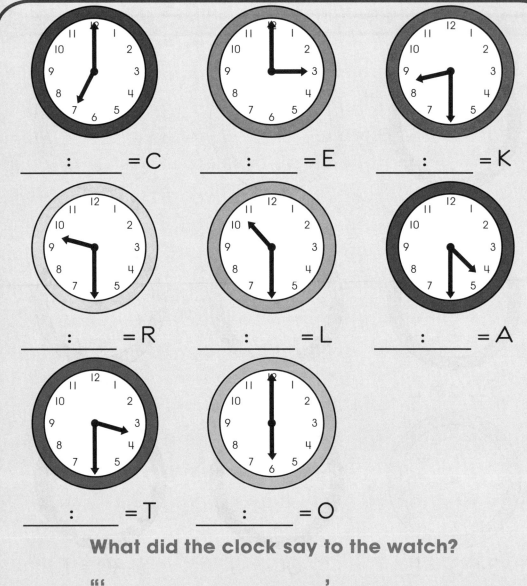

____ : ____ = C

____ : ____ = E

____ : ____ = K

____ : ____ = R

____ : ____ = L

____ : ____ = A

____ : ____ = T

____ : ____ = O

What did the clock say to the watch?

" ____ ____ ____ ____ , ____ ____
  3:30 6:00 7:00 8:30   3:30 6:00

you ____ ____ ____ ____ ____ "
     10:30 4:30 3:30 3:00 9:30

CD-104367

Draw lines to connect the clocks that show the same time.

 CD-104367 **15**

Solve each word problem. Match the answers to the times and numbers below. Write the correct letters on the lines.

1. Jay left for school at 7:30. He got to school at 7:40. How long did it take him to get there?

    I

2. It takes Kasey 15 minutes to eat breakfast. If she starts eating at 8:30, what time will she finish?

    T

3. Bailey played soccer after school. The game started at 3:00. It lasted 2 hours. What time did the game end?

    U

4. Liza spent 45 minutes doing her homework. She finished at 4:30. What time did she start?

    M

5. Music lessons last for 25 minutes. If a lesson begins at 9:20, what time does it end?

    N

6. Tavaris read for 10 minutes. He practiced math for 15 minutes. He studied spelling for 10 minutes. How long did he work?

    E

There are 1,440 of these in one day.

_____ _____ _____ _____ _____ _____ S
3:45   10 min.   9:45   5:00   8:45   35 min.

Use the calendar to answer each question.

May

Sunday	Monday	Tuesday	Wednesday	Thursday	Friday	Saturday
		1	2	3	4 soccer practice	5	6
7	8 music lesson	9	10	11 soccer practice	12	13 beach party
14	15	16 Lisa's birthday	17	18 soccer practice	19	20
21	22	23	24 pizza party	25 soccer practice	26 family picnic	27
28	29	30	31			

1. On what day is the music lesson? _____

2. How many Thursdays are in this month? _____

3. The 31st is on a _____.

4. What date is the Friday before the beach party? _____

5. When is Lisa's birthday? _____

6. What event is planned for the 24th? _____ _____

7. The beach party is _____ days after the music lesson.

8. What takes place every Thursday?_____

Read the poem. Then, follow the directions to complete the calendar and discover which month it is.

Sunday						

Thirty days has September, April, June, and November. All the rest have 31, except February, which stands alone.

1. Write the rest of the days of the week on the calendar.

2. This month starts on a Tuesday and ends on a Thursday. Number the calendar days.

3. This month has a holiday on Friday the 25th this year. Draw a star to mark the holiday.

4. What month is this? _____

Color the days from the list on the calendar to see a picture.

Special Days This Month
Mom's birthday: 1st
Soccer game: 3rd
Report due: last Friday of the month
Dentist appointment: 16th
Grandma's visit: 29th–31st
No school: 21st

OCTOBER

Sunday	Monday	Tuesday	Wednesday	Thursday	Friday	Saturday
		1	2	3	4	5
6	7	8	9	10	11	12
13	14	15	16	17	18	19
20	21	22	23	24	25	26
27	28	29	30	31		

Solve each problem. Color the apple in each bowl that shows the correct answer.

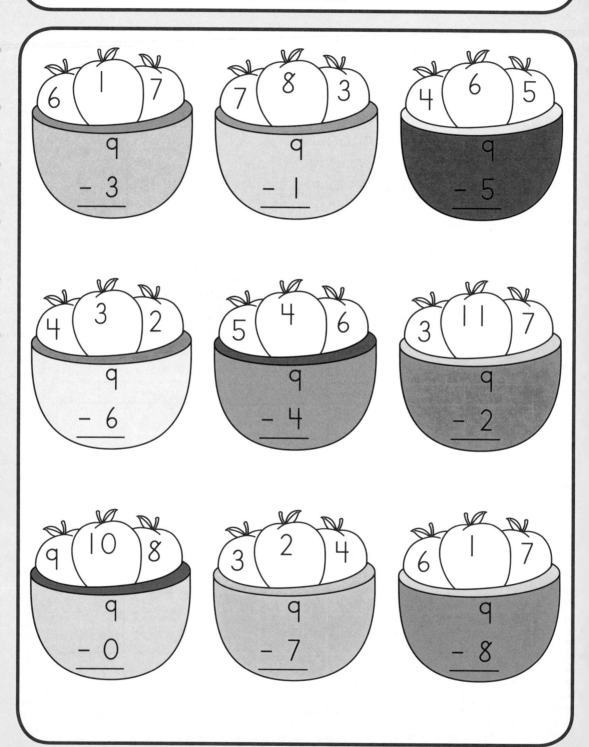

CD-104367
© Carson-Dellosa

Solve each problem. Draw an X on each baseball if its answer is an even number.

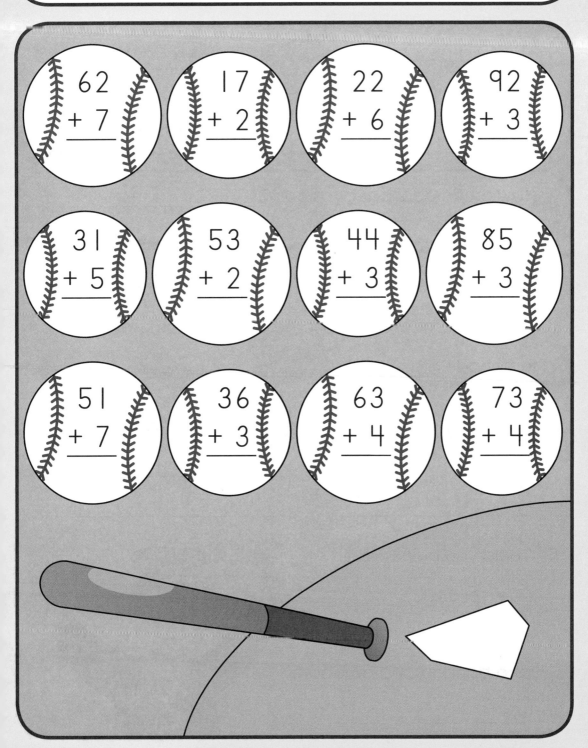

$$62 + 7$$

$$17 + 2$$

$$22 + 6$$

$$92 + 3$$

$$31 + 5$$

$$53 + 2$$

$$44 + 3$$

$$85 + 3$$

$$51 + 7$$

$$36 + 3$$

$$63 + 4$$

$$73 + 4$$

CD-104367

Use the menu to answer each question.

Menu

piece of pie $0.75	banana $0.75
pizza slice $1.25	lemonade $0.50
ice cream..............$0.50	apple $0.25
pretzel....................$0.25	baby carrots $1.00

1. How much do 2 bananas cost?_____

2. How much does it cost for a piece of pie and lemonade?

   _____

3. Which 2 items added together cost the same as

   lemonade?_____

4. List 3 groups of 3 items that you could buy for $1.75.

   _____

   _____

5. Could you buy 3 pizza

   slices for $3.00? _____

6. How much does it cost
   for a banana and an apple?

   _____

Write three addition sentences for the sum shown on each roof.

11

___ + ___ = 11
___ + ___ = 11
___ + ___ = 11

12

___ + ___ = 12
___ + ___ = 12
___ + ___ = 12

13

___ + ___ = 13
___ + ___ = 13
___ + ___ = 13

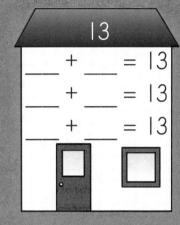

14

___ + ___ = 14
___ + ___ = 14
___ + ___ = 14

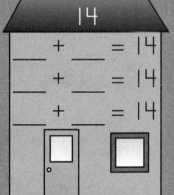

15

___ + ___ = 15
___ + ___ = 15
___ + ___ = 15

16

___ + ___ = 16
___ + ___ = 16
___ + ___ = 16

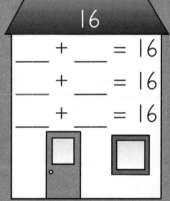

17

___ + ___ = 17
___ + ___ = 17
___ + ___ = 17

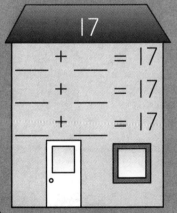

18

___ + ___ = 18
___ + ___ = 18
___ + ___ = 18

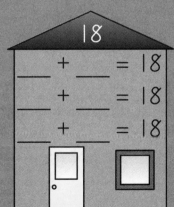

19

___ + ___ = 19
___ + ___ = 19
___ + ___ = 19

CD-104367

Check each answer. Draw an X on each incorrect answer to pop the balloon.

$$85 - 71 = 14$$

$$63 - 21 = 44$$

$$36 - 22 = 58$$

$$94 - 81 = 13$$

$$45 - 21 = 64$$

$$67 - 34 = 33$$

$$76 - 61 = 15$$

$$24 - 13 = 11$$

$$57 - 25 = 23$$

CD-104367

Play tic-tac-toe. Solve each problem. Draw an X on each answer that is an even number. Draw an O on each answer that is an odd number.

6 + 3 + 2 =	2 + 2 + 2 =	1 + 3 + 2 =
4 + 3 + 0 =	0 + 6 + 3 =	4 + 3 + 3 =
2 + 2 + 4 =	3 + 1 + 5 =	0 + 7 + 1 =
2 + 6 + 2 =	4 + 3 + 2 =	4 + 4 + 2 =
1 + 5 + 1 =	1 + 4 + 3 =	6 + 3 + 1 =
2 + 4 + 2 =	3 + 3 + 3 =	0 + 5 + 2 =

Solve each problem. Use the key to color the butterfly.

400-499 = **green**   500-599 = **pink**   600-699 = **blue**
700-799 = **orange** 800-899 = **yellow**

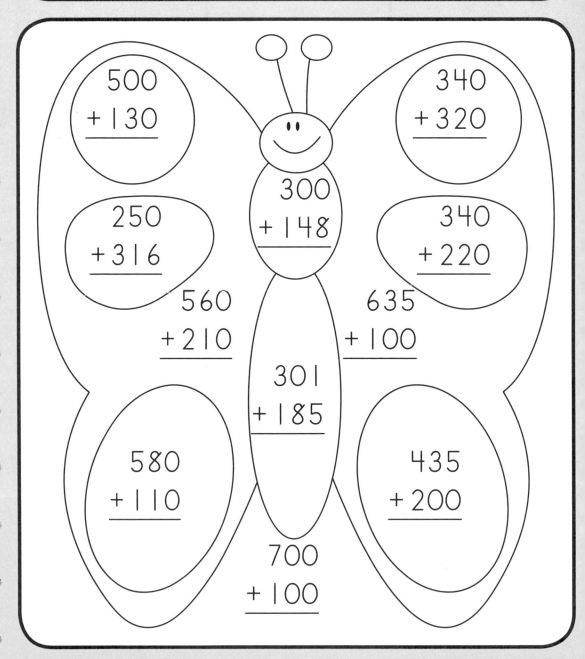

$$500 + 130$$

$$340 + 320$$

$$250 + 316$$

$$300 + 148$$

$$340 + 220$$

$$560 + 210$$

$$635 + 100$$

$$301 + 185$$

$$580 + 110$$

$$435 + 200$$

$$700 + 100$$

CD-104367

Cut the page on the dotted line. Give half to a friend. Who can solve the problems faster?

GO!

7	8	9	6
+ 5	+ 9	+ 5	+ 7

8	9	7	9	8
+ 8	+ 6	+ 8	+ 8	+ 7

6	8	7	8	9
+ 9	+ 5	+ 9	+ 6	+ 7

- -

GO!

7	8	9	6
+ 5	+ 9	+ 5	+ 7

8	9	7	9	8
+ 8	+ 6	+ 8	+ 8	+ 7

6	8	7	8	9
+ 9	+ 5	+ 9	+ 6	+ 7

Cut the page on the dotted line. Give half to a friend. Who can solve the problems faster?

GO!

14 − 5	17 − 8	12 − 5	18 − 9
14 − 8	14 − 7	13 − 9	16 − 8	15 − 9
13 − 5	14 − 9	11 − 6	14 − 6	11 − 9

- - - - - - - - - - - - - - - - - - - -

GO!

14 − 5	17 − 8	12 − 5	18 − 9
14 − 8	14 − 7	13 − 9	16 − 8	15 − 9
13 − 5	14 − 9	11 − 6	14 − 6	11 − 9

Solve each problem. Write the answers to complete the puzzle.

Across

1. $23 + 41 =$

3. $8 + 4 =$

4. $649 - 112 =$

6. $55 + 5 =$

7. $2,799 - 1,560 =$

9. $998 - 384 =$

Down

2. $130 + 320 =$

3. $110 + 63 =$

5. $50 + 21 =$

6. $896 - 215 =$

8. $198 - 101 =$

Write the fraction for the part of each pizza that has toppings.

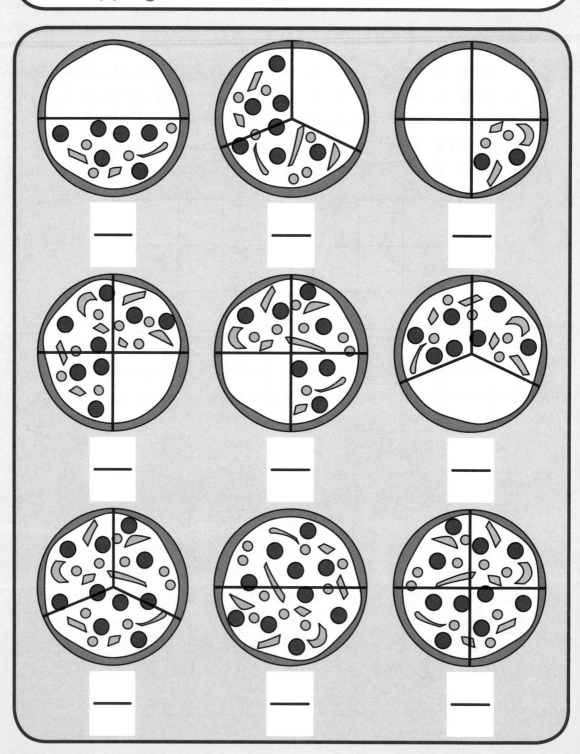

CD-104367   © Carson-Dellosa

Page 1
The picture should show a woman driving a tractor.

Page 2
red: 2 + 0 = 2; yellow: 2 + 2 = 4;
blue: 3 + 3 = 6; 4 + 2 = 6;
orange: 5 + 2 = 7;
green: 5 + 3 = 8; 4 + 4 = 8;
purple: 4 + 6 = 10

Page 3
Row 1: 5, 1, 6, 6; Row 2: 6, 6, 0, 2;
Row 3: 8, 7, 3, 9; Row 4: 4, 3, 11, 10;
The blue whale

Page 4
1. fish; 2. one; 3. octopuses; 4. twenty;
A foot

Page 5
1. 13; 2. 7; 3. 6; 4. 11; 5. 8; 6. 17;
In a school

Page 6
Row 1: 47, 68, 97, 39, 76;
Row 2: 54, 54, 47, 68, 97;
Row 3: 97, 47, 76, 39;
Row 4: 76, 54, 97, 68
Bunch with number 97 under it should be circled.

Page 7
Row 1: 9, 9, 6, 9; Row 2: 6, 2, 8, 7, 7;
Row 3: 8, 6, 4, 8, 6

Page 8
Row 1: 3, 6, 2, 0, 1; Row 2: 1, 6, 2, 3, 4;
Row 3: 2, 6, 5, 5

Page 9
Row 1: 8, 3, 2; Row 2: 5, 7, 5, 0, 4;
Row 3: 3, 6, 2, 2, 3; Row 4: 3, 1, 5, 2

Page 10
red: 7__2__; 9__20__; 5__7__; 13__9__; 65__4__
blue: 146; 4__60__; __61__; 5__00__; 7__25__; 9__62__
green: __398__; __7__44; __9__07

Page 11
Row 1: 9, 6, 8; Row 2: 8, 8, 6;
Row 3: 9, 7, 9; Row 4 : 7, 8, 9;
Row 5: 7, 5, 6; Row 6: 7, 7, 8

Page 11, continued

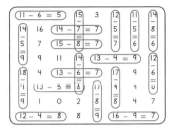

Page 12
Row 1: 20; Row 2: 60, 80, 90;
Row: 3: 4, 6, 10; Row 4: 12, 18;
Row 5: 15, 20; Row 6: 30, 45;
Row 7: 55, 60, 65; Row 8: 3, 12;
Row 9: 18, 21; Row 10: 27, 33

Page 13

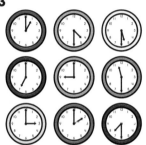

"Time Flies"

Page 14
7:00 = C; 3:00 = E; 8:30 = K; 9:30 = R;
10:30 = L; 4:30 = A; 3:30 = T;
6:00 = O; "'Tock' to you later!"

Page 15

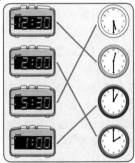

Page 16
1. 10 minutes; 2. 8:45; 3. 5:00; 4. 3:45;
5. 9:45; 6. 35 minutes, Minutes

Page 17
1. Monday; 2. 4; 3. Wednesday; 4. 12th;
5. Tuesday the 16th; 6. pizza party; 7. 5;
8. soccer practice

Page 18
Calendar should be filled in correctly.;
December

Page 19
The picture should show a smiley face.

Page 20
Row 1: 6, 8, and 4 should be colored.
Row 2: 3, 5, and 7 should be colored.
Row 3: 9, 2, and 1 should be colored.

Page 21
Row 1: 69, 19, 28, 95;
Row 2: 36, 55, 47, 88;
Row 3: 58, 39, 67, 77

Page 22
1. $1.50; 2. $1.25; 3. apple and pretzel;
4. Answers will vary but should add up
to $1.75.; 5. no; 6. $1.00

Page 23
Answers will vary but may include:
11: 11 + 0, 10 + 1, 9 + 2, 8 + 3, 7 + 4,
6 + 5;
12: 12 + 0, 11 + 1, 10 + 2, 9 + 3, 8 + 4,
7 + 5, 6 + 6;
13: 13 + 0, 12 + 1, 11 + 2, 10 + 3, 9 + 4,
8 + 5, 7 + 6;
14: 14 + 0, 13 + 1, 12 + 2, 11 + 3, 10 + 4,
9 + 5, 8 + 6, 7 + 7;
15: 15 + 0, 14 + 1, 13 + 2, 12 + 3, 11 + 4,
10 + 5, 9 + 6, 8 + 7;
16: 16 + 0, 15 + 1, 14 + 2, 13 + 3, 12 + 4,
11 + 5, 10 + 6, 9 + 7, 8 + 8;
17: 17 + 0, 16 + 1, 15 + 2, 14 + 3, 13 + 4,
12 + 5, 11 + 6, 10 + 7, 9 + 8;
18: 18 + 0, 17 + 1, 16 + 2, 15 + 3, 14 + 4,
13 + 5, 12 + 6, 11 + 7, 10 + 8, 9 + 9;
19: 19 + 0, 18 + 1, 17 + 2, 16 + 3, 15 + 4,
14 + 5, 13 + 6, 12 + 7, 11 + 8, 10 + 9

Page 24
Xs should be drawn on the balloons with
the following answers: 44, 58, 64, 23

Page 25
Row 1: 11, 6, 6; Row 2: 7, 9, 10;
Row 3: 8, 9, 8; Tic-tac-toe is formed
vertically through 6, 10, 8;
Row 4: 10, 9, 10; Row 5: 7, 8, 10;
Row 6: 8, 9, 7; Tic-tac-toe is formed
diagonally through 8, 8, 10.

Page 26
From left to right and top to bottom:
630, 660, 566, 448, 560, 770, 735, 486,
690, 635, 800; Check that the butterfly
is colored correctly.

Page 27
Row 1: 12, 17, 14, 13;
Row 2: 16, 15, 15, 17, 15;
Row 3: 15, 13, 16, 14, 16

Page 28
Row 1: 9, 9, 7, 9;
Row 2: 6, 7, 4, 8, 6;
Row 3: 8, 5, 5, 8, 2

Page 29
Across: 1. 64; 3. 12; 4. 537; 6. 60;
7. 1,239; 9. 614;
Down: 2. 450; 3. 173; 5. 71; 6. 681;
8. 97

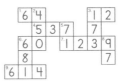

Page 30
Row 1: $\frac{1}{2}$; $\frac{2}{3}$; $\frac{1}{4}$
Row 2: $\frac{3}{4}$; $\frac{3}{4}$; $\frac{2}{3}$
Row 3: $\frac{3}{3}$; $\frac{2}{2}$; $\frac{4}{4}$

Page 31
C = $\frac{1}{3}$, H = $\frac{1}{2}$, E = $\frac{2}{3}$, S = $\frac{1}{4}$, Cheese

Page 32
Kittens

Page 33

⊞ = green

▥ , ◔ = yellow

⊟ , ◑ = red

⊞ , ⊕ = blue

Check that the robot is colored correctly.

Page 34

The picture should show a dollar sign.

Page 35

7¢, 17¢, 9¢, 20¢, 21¢, 30¢, 16¢, 40¢,

Just one "scent"

Page 36

Answers will vary but may include:

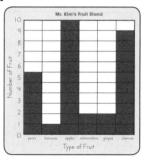

Page 37

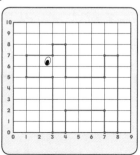

Page 38

1. dog, 2. dog, 3. turtle, 4. hamster,
5. horse, 6. Answers will vary.

Page 39

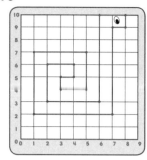

Page 40

Page 41

1. 10, 2. 12, 3. 12, 4. 15

Page 42

1. drums; 2. $30.00; 3. $112.00;
4. cymbals, guitar, saxophone;
5. $90.00; 6. $40.00

Page 43

1. 335, see; 2. 7714, hill; 3. 57738, bells;
4. 3045, shoe; 5. 35006, goose;
6. 38076, globe; 7. 77345, shell;
8. 14, hi

Page 44

Row 1: 90, 82, 92, 93;

Row 2: 45, 60, 96, 35;

Row 3: 94, 25, 89, 80;

Row 4: 91, 51, 71, 64;

Fun in the sun!

Page 45

The picture should show a camera and photos.

Page 46

1. Henry; 2. Haley; 3. Ben; 4. Camden

Page 47

1. Libby; 2. Anton; 3. Amad; 4. Molly

Page 48

Ariel: 2, 7, 5, 5, 6, 9, 10, 9, 8, 10, 8, 7;

Wesley: 10, 7, 7, 7, 4, 9, 4, 6, 9, 8, 6, 6;

Tina: 7, 3, 10, 9, 10, 7, 7, 9, 3, 6, 9, 4

Page 49

sunglasses: $1\frac{1}{2}$ in.; shovel: 3 in.;

bucket: $2\frac{1}{2}$ in.; sand castle: 4 in.;

crab: 2 in.; water: 1 in.; Good work

Page 50
Row I: 9, 33, 78, 48;
Row 2: 26, 49, 34, 46;
Row 3: 39, 24, 58, 18;
All eggs should be colored.

Page 51
1. 68 − 29 = 39, 39 + 29 = 68,
2. 62 − 33 = 29, 29 + 33 = 62,
3. 75 − 17 = 58, 58 + 17 = 75,
4. 81 − 13 = 68, 68 + 13 = 81,
5. 35 − 17 = 18, 18 + 17 = 35,
6. 86 − 49 = 37, 37 + 49 = 86,
7. 81 − 29 = 52, 52 + 29 = 81,
8. 66 − 17 = 49, 49 + 17 = 66,
9. 94 − 25 = 69, 69 + 25 = 94,
10. 41 − 13 = 28, 28 + 13 = 41
Dino–mite!

Page 52
1. >, 2. <, 3. >, 4. >, 5. <, 6. >, 7. <,
8. >, 9. <, 10. <, 11. >, 12. >
Donkey, monkey

Page 53
From left to right and top to bottom:
8, 3, 9, 6, 1, 7, 1, 2, 4; A dino sore

Page 54
2 + 3 + 5 = 10, 3 + 6 + 7 = 16,
9 + 1 + 3 = 13, 6 + 5 + 6 = 17,
4 + 6 + 2 = 12, 3 + 4 + 1 = 8,
3 + 7 + 4 = 14, 6 + 2 + 1 = 9,
6 + 6 + 9 = 21; Check that flowers are colored correctly.

Page 55
1. 55, 56, 57, 58, 59;
2. 10, 11, 15, 16, 19;
3. 43, 67, 69, 70, 82;
4. 92, 93, 97, 101, 105

Page 56
From left to right and top to bottom:
10 x 1 = 10, 5 x 2 = 10, 2 x 2 = 4,
4 x 1 = 4, 2 x 5 = 10, 1 x 5 = 5, 5 x 1 = 5,
12 x 1 = 12, 1 x 10 = 10, 4 x 3 = 12,
1 x 10 = 10, 3 x 4 = 12, 2 x 6 = 12,
2 x 5 = 10, 6 x 2 = 12, 1 x 12 = 12,
5 x 2 = 10, 1 x 6 = 6, 3 x 2 = 6,
4 x 3= 12, 12 x 1 = 12, 3 x 4 = 12,
3 x 2 = 6, 6 x 1 = 6, 2 x 6 = 12
The picture should show a sand castle.

Page 57
1. M, 2. U, 3. S, 4. H, 5. R, 6. O, 7. O,
8. M, Mushroom

Page 58
Rocket 1: 10, 9, 8, 7, 6, 5, 4, 3, 2, 1
Rocket 2: 50, 45, 40, 35, 30, 25, 20, 15, 10
Rocket 3: 20, 18, 16, 14, 12, 10, 8, 6, 4, 2

Page 59
1. 4:00 P.M., 2. nighttime; 3. 2 hours;
4. 7 hours; 5. 7 hours;
6. Answers will vary.

Page 60
Row I: 37, 5, 72, 7;
Row 2: 62, 49, 25, 87;
Row 3: 2, 91, 33, 57; An elephant's shadow

Write the fraction for the part of each pizza that remains. Match the answers to the fractions below. Write the correct letters on the lines.

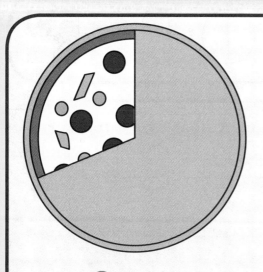

C = ——

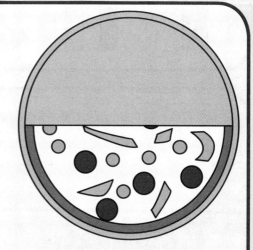

H = ——

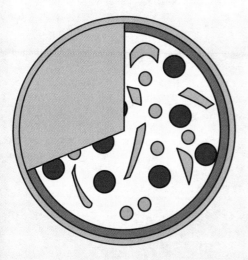

E = ——

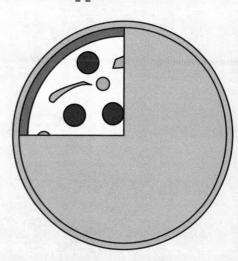

S = ——

What kind of pizza likes to have its picture taken?

—— —— —— —— —— ——

$\frac{1}{3}$ $\frac{1}{2}$ $\frac{2}{3}$ $\frac{2}{3}$ $\frac{1}{4}$ $\frac{2}{3}$

Match each fraction picture to its fraction below. Write the correct letters on the lines.

N= K= E= T= I= S=

What does a cat have that no other animal has?

___ ___ ___ ___ ___ ___ ___

$\frac{1}{3}$ $\frac{1}{4}$ $\frac{2}{2}$ $\frac{2}{2}$ $\frac{2}{3}$ $\frac{1}{2}$ $\frac{3}{4}$

 CD-104367

Use the key to color the picture.

$\frac{4}{4}$ = green $\frac{2}{3}$ = yellow $\frac{1}{2}$ = red $\frac{1}{4}$ = blue

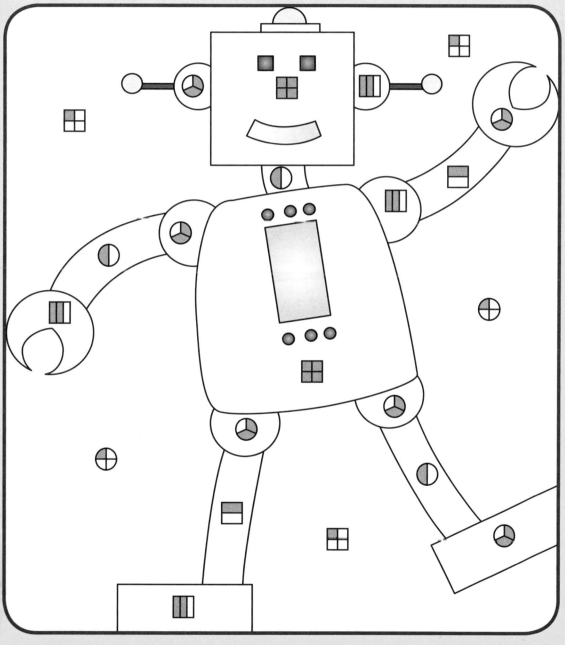

Color each space that shows a coin combination that equals 50 cents.

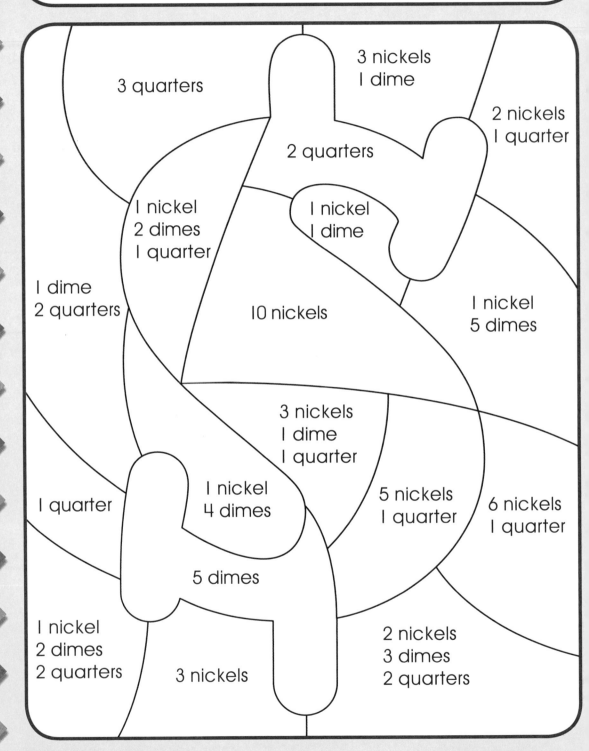

3 quarters

3 nickels
1 dime

2 nickels
1 quarter

2 quarters

1 nickel
2 dimes
1 quarter

1 nickel
1 dime

1 dime
2 quarters

10 nickels

1 nickel
5 dimes

3 nickels
1 dime
1 quarter

1 quarter

1 nickel
4 dimes

5 nickels
1 quarter

6 nickels
1 quarter

5 dimes

1 nickel
2 dimes
2 quarters

3 nickels

2 nickels
3 dimes
2 quarters

CD-104367

Add the values listed in each box. Match the answers to the amounts below. Write the correct letters on the lines.

one nickel two pennies _____ ¢ <div align="right">T</div>	one dime one nickel two pennies _____ ¢ <div align="right">J</div>
one nickel four pennies _____ ¢ <div align="right">C</div>	four nickels _____ ¢ <div align="right">O</div>
two dimes one penny _____ ¢ <div align="right">E</div>	two nickels two dimes _____ ¢ <div align="right">S</div>
one dime one nickel one penny _____ ¢ <div align="right">N</div>	four dimes _____ ¢ <div align="right">U</div>

How much is a skunk worth?

____ ____ ____ ____   ____ ____ ____   " ____ ____ ____ ____ ____ "
17¢ 40¢ 30¢ 7¢   20¢ 16¢ 21¢   30¢ 9¢ 21¢ 16¢ 7¢

CD-104367 **35**

Write a number in each box. When the numbers are added across and down, they should equal the sums next to each row and column. The first one has been done for you.

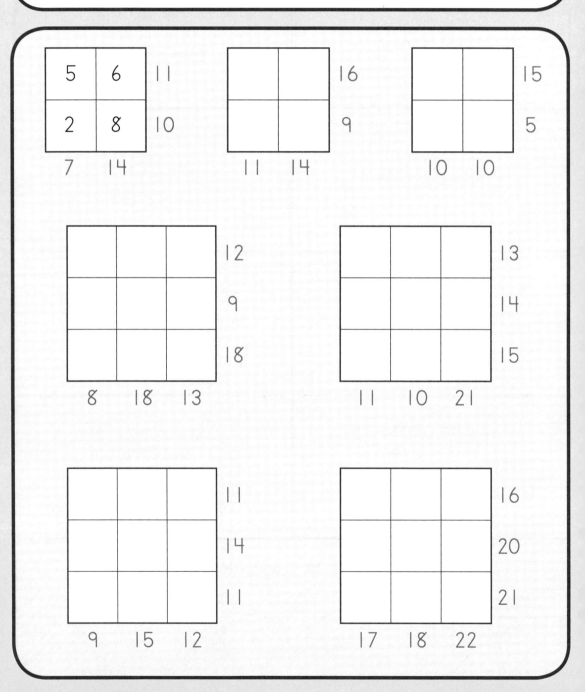

5	6	11
2	8	10
7	14	

		16
		9
11	14	

		15
		5
10	10	

			12
			9
			18
8	18	13	

			13
			14
			15
11	10	21	

			11
			14
			11
9	15	12	

			16
			20
			21
17	18	22	

Use the information to complete the graph.

5 pears   I banana   10 apples
2 watermelons   2 bunches of grapes   9 cherries

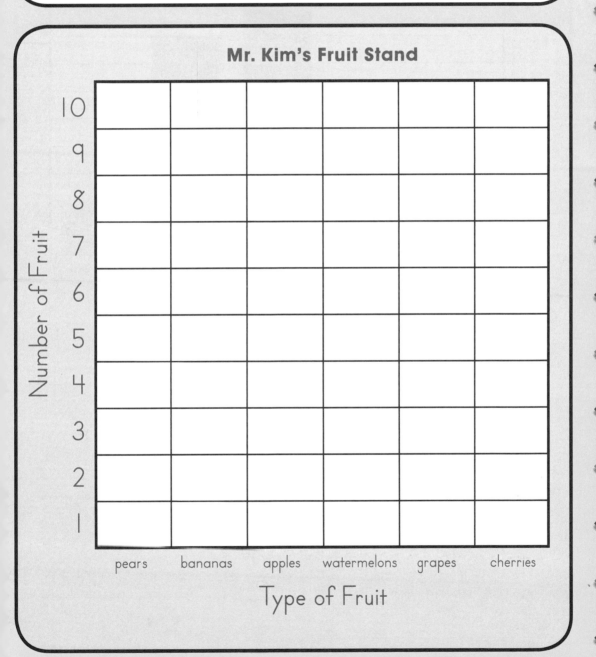

Mr. Kim's Fruit Stand

Number of Fruit

10
9
8
7
6
5
4
3
2
1

pears   bananas   apples   watermelons   grapes   cherries

Type of Fruit

Use the graph to answer each question.

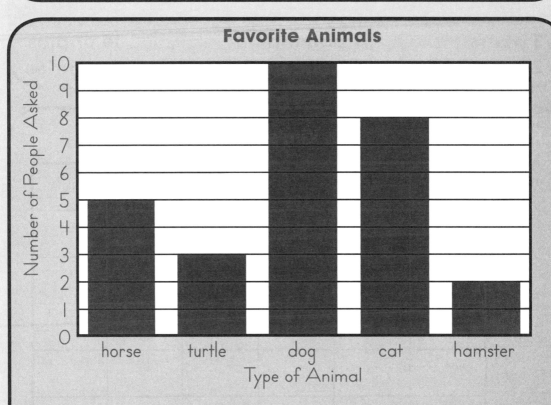

Favorite Animals

1. Did more people name dog or cat as their favorite animal?

   _____

2. The most people named this animal as their favorite.

   _____

3. Did more people name hamster or turtle as their favorite animal?

   _____

4. The fewest people named this animal as their favorite.

   _____

5. Five people named this animal as their favorite.

   _____

6. What is your favorite animal?

   _____

Plot each coordinate on the graph. Connect the points in order. The first two have been connected for you.

Coordinates

(1,7); (3,7); (3,8); (4,8); (4,5); (7,5); (7,7); (8,7); (8,0);
(7,0); (7,2); (4,2); (4,0); (3,0); (3,5); (1,5); (1,7)

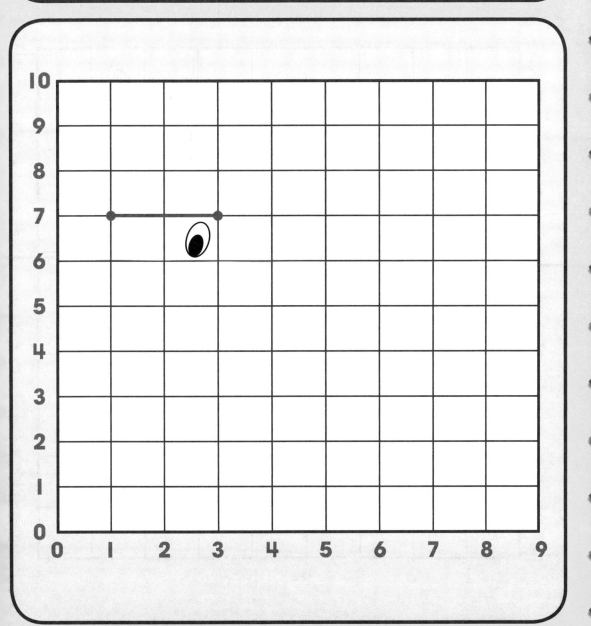

Plot each coordinate on the graph. Connect the points in order.

Coordinates
(6,10); (8,10); (8,9); (7,9); (7,2); (1,2); (1,7); (5,7); (5,4); (3,4); (3,5); (4,5); (4,6); (2,6); (2,3); (6,3); (6,10)

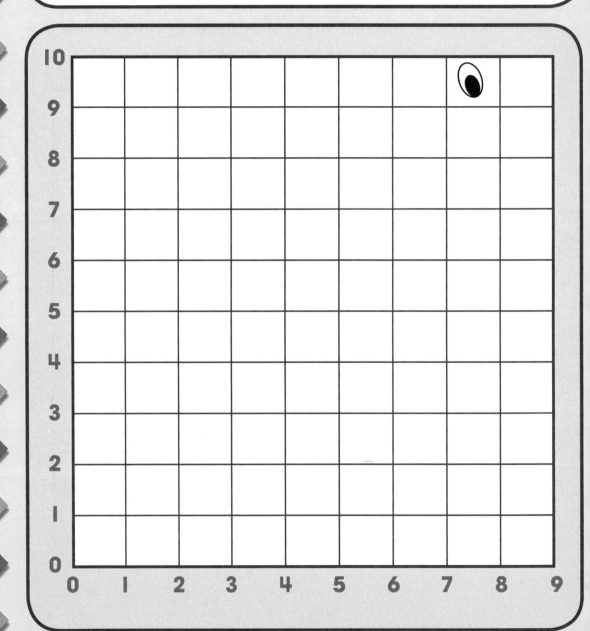

CD-104367 © Carson-Dellosa

Solve each word problem.

1. Each vase holds 5 flowers. Molly needs to fill 2 vases. How many flowers does Molly need?_____

2. The flower shop has 3 flowerpots. Each flowerpot has 4 flowers in it. How many flowers are in the pots altogether? _____

3. The flower shop has 2 empty shelves. If the owner buys 6 vases for each shelf, how many total vases does he buy? _____

4. The flower shop received a shipment of new flowers. There were 5 daises, 5 roses, and 5 carnations. How many new flowers were there in all? _____

Use the price list to answer each question.

Price List

flute $70.00	drums $100.00
guitar..................$35.00	cymbals $25.00
saxophone.........$50.00	drumsticks............$12.00
music lesson $10.00	

1. Which instrument is the most expensive? _____

2. Jana wants to learn to play the guitar. If each music lesson is $10.00, how much will she pay for 3 lessons?

   _____

3. Anthony wants to buy drums and drumsticks. How much money does he need? _____

4. Valerie has $50.00. What instruments could she buy for $50.00 or less? _____

   _____

5. How much would Grant pay for a flute and 2 music lessons? _____

6. If the owner of the music store took $10.00 off the price of the saxophone, how much would it cost? _____

   _____

Use a calculator to solve each problem. Write the answer, then turn the calculator upside down. Write the secret word.

1. $279 + 56 =$

_____

_____

2. $8,366 - 652 =$

_____

_____

3. $39,587 + 18,151 =$

_____

_____

4. $1,563 + 1,482 =$

_____

_____

5. $30,438 + 4,568 =$

_____

_____

6. $25,450 + 12,626 =$

_____

_____

7. $74,325 + 3,020 =$

_____

_____

8. $959 - 945 =$

_____

_____

Make your own upside-down messages!

I = I   4 = H   6 = G   8 = B   3 = E   5 = S   7 = L   0 = O

Solve each problem. Match the answers to the numbers below. Write the correct letters on the lines.

78 +12 T	36 +46 E	65 +27 U	54 +39 I
27 +18 N	33 +27 F	48 +48 N	17 +18 !
85 + 9 U	17 + 8 H	61 +28 O	51 +29 A
77 +14 S	24 +27 T	33 +38 N	45 +19 C

What is a good time in the sun?

___ ___ ___   ___ ___
60   94   45   93   96

___ ___ ___   ___ ___ ___ ___
51   25   82   91   92   71   35

CD-104367

Connect the dots from 3 to 39. Count by 3s. Start at the ★. Color the picture.

Henry, Ben, Camden, and Haley are flying kites. Use the clues to decide which kite belongs to each child. Write each child's name beside the correct kite.

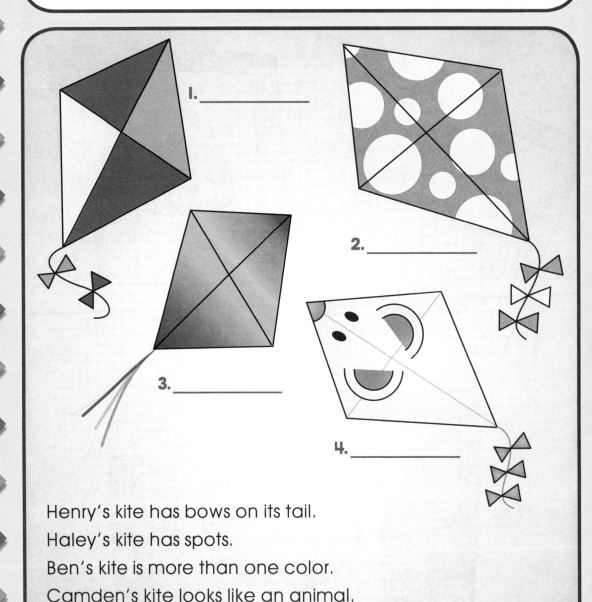

1. _____

2. _____

3. _____

4. _____

Henry's kite has bows on its tail.

Haley's kite has spots.

Ben's kite is more than one color.

Camden's kite looks like an animal.

Amad, Molly, Anton, and Libby each brought a ball to the beach. Use the clues to decide who brought each ball. Write each child's name beside the correct ball.

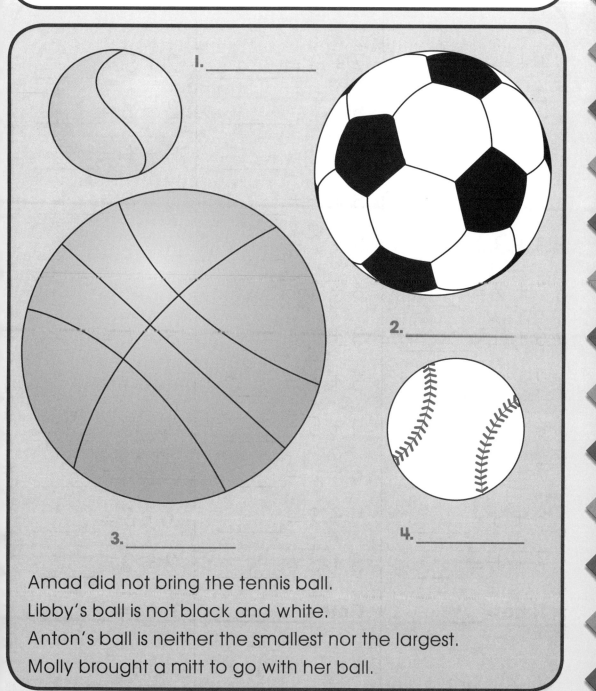

1._____

2._____

3._____

4._____

Amad did not bring the tennis ball.
Libby's ball is not black and white.
Anton's ball is neither the smallest nor the largest.
Molly brought a mitt to go with her ball.

CD-104367

47

Ariel, Wesley, and Tina are having a race to see who can swim the fastest. Solve the problems. Time yourself. Record your times to find the winner.

Ariel	Wesley	Tina
1 + 1 = ____	7 + 3 = ____	2 + 5 = ____
5 + 2 = ____	6 + 1 = ____	2 + 1 = ____
3 + 2 = ____	5 + 2 = ____	9 + 1 = ____
4 + 1 = ____	3 + 4 = ____	3 + 6 = ____
3 + 3 = ____	2 + 2 = ____	5 + 5 = ____
7 + 2 = ____	6 + 3 = ____	5 + 2 = ____
6 + 4 = ____	3 + 1 = ____	6 + 1 = ____
4 + 5 = ____	5 + 1 = ____	4 + 5 = ____
6 + 2 = ____	4 + 5 = ____	3 + 0 = ____
7 + 3 = ____	6 + 2 = ____	0 + 6 = ____
5 + 3 = ____	4 + 2 = ____	1 + 8 = ____
6 + 1 = ____	3 + 3 = ____	2 + 2 = ____
Time = _____	Time = _____	Time = _____

CD-104367

Use a ruler to measure each picture in inches. Match the answers to the measurements below. Write the correct bold letters on the lines.

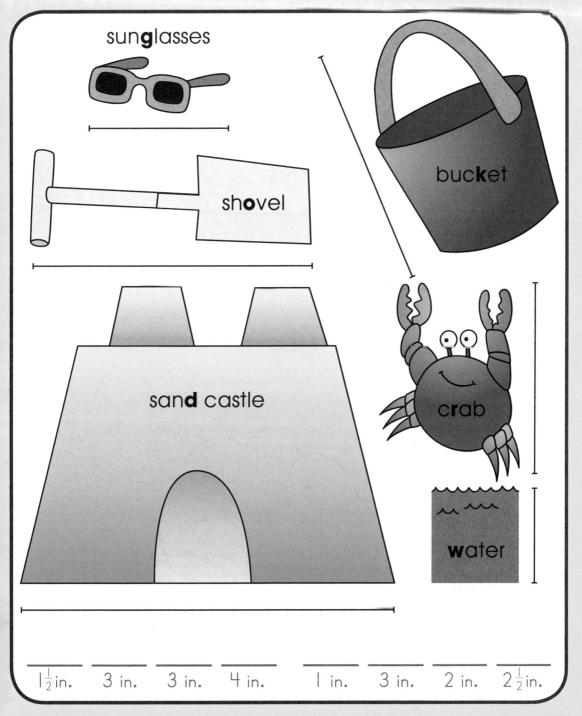

sun**g**lasses

bucket

sh**o**vel

san**d** castle

c**r**ab

water

| $1\frac{1}{2}$ in. | 3 in. | 3 in. | 4 in. | 1 in. | 3 in. | 2 in. | $2\frac{1}{2}$ in. |

Solve each problem. Then, color the egg that matches the answer.

$$\begin{array}{r} 41 \\ -32 \\ \hline \end{array}$$
$$\begin{array}{r} 51 \\ -18 \\ \hline \end{array}$$
$$\begin{array}{r} 94 \\ -16 \\ \hline \end{array}$$
$$\begin{array}{r} 76 \\ -28 \\ \hline \end{array}$$

$$\begin{array}{r} 84 \\ -58 \\ \hline \end{array}$$
$$\begin{array}{r} 87 \\ -38 \\ \hline \end{array}$$
$$\begin{array}{r} 62 \\ -28 \\ \hline \end{array}$$
$$\begin{array}{r} 92 \\ -46 \\ \hline \end{array}$$

$$\begin{array}{r} 74 \\ -35 \\ \hline \end{array}$$
$$\begin{array}{r} 81 \\ -57 \\ \hline \end{array}$$
$$\begin{array}{r} 85 \\ -27 \\ \hline \end{array}$$
$$\begin{array}{r} 53 \\ -35 \\ \hline \end{array}$$

26 9 49 18 24
34 33 39
48 58 78 46

Solve each problem. Use addition to check each answer. Match the answers to numbers below. Write the correct letters on the lines.

1. $\begin{array}{r} 68 \\ -29 \\ \hline 39 \end{array}$ D $\begin{array}{r} 39 \\ +29 \\ \hline 68 \end{array}$

2. $\begin{array}{r} 62 \\ -33 \\ \hline \end{array}$ M $\begin{array}{r} \\ + \\ \hline \end{array}$

3. $\begin{array}{r} 75 \\ -17 \\ \hline \end{array}$ K $\begin{array}{r} \\ + \\ \hline \end{array}$

4. $\begin{array}{r} 81 \\ -13 \\ \hline \end{array}$ I $\begin{array}{r} \\ + \\ \hline \end{array}$

5. $\begin{array}{r} 35 \\ -17 \\ \hline \end{array}$ I $\begin{array}{r} \\ + \\ \hline \end{array}$

6. $\begin{array}{r} 86 \\ -49 \\ \hline \end{array}$ N $\begin{array}{r} \\ + \\ \hline \end{array}$

7. $\begin{array}{r} 81 \\ -29 \\ \hline \end{array}$ O $\begin{array}{r} \\ + \\ \hline \end{array}$

8. $\begin{array}{r} 66 \\ -17 \\ \hline \end{array}$ F $\begin{array}{r} \\ + \\ \hline \end{array}$

9. $\begin{array}{r} 94 \\ -25 \\ \hline \end{array}$ T $\begin{array}{r} \\ + \\ \hline \end{array}$

10. $\begin{array}{r} 41 \\ -13 \\ \hline \end{array}$ E $\begin{array}{r} \\ + \\ \hline \end{array}$

$\underset{39}{\text{D}}$ $\underset{18}{\quad}$ $\underset{37}{\quad}$ $\underset{52}{\quad}$ $-$ $\underset{29}{\quad}$ $\underset{68}{\quad}$ $\underset{69}{\quad}$ $\underset{28}{\quad}$!

Write < or > in each box. Circle the letter beside the greater number in each number pair. To solve the riddle, write the circled letters in order on the lines.

1. D 741 ☐ 714 Q   2. P   27 ☐ 28 O

3. N 658 ☐ 642 E   4. K 605 ☐ 65 O

5. S   73 ☐ 79 E   6. Y 301 ☐ 300 N

7. R   15 ☐ 22 M   8. O 236 ☐ 233 L

9. B   64 ☐ 73 N   10. C   36 ☐ 42 K

11. E 321 ☐ 231 P   12. Y   49 ☐ 39 K

What keys cannot open any doors?

___ ___ ___ ___ ___ ___

___ ___ ___ ___ ___

Solve each problem. Write each answer under the problem. Use the code to write the correct letter under each answer.

1=**O**   2=**R**   3=**D**   4=**E**   5=**D**   6=**N**   7=**S**   8=**A**   9=**I**

What do you call a lizard's big cut?

16 − 8	11 − 8	18 − 9	12 − 6	10 − 9

14 − 7	7 − 6	10 − 8	12 − 8

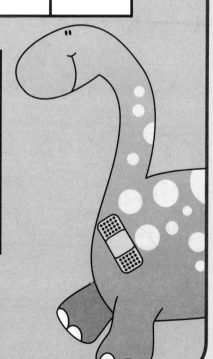

   CD-104367   **53**

Solve each problem. Find each sum in a smaller flower. Color each problem flower and its answer flower a matching color.

2
3
+ 5

3
6
+ 7

12

14

4
6
+ 2

9

21

9
1
+ 3

6
5
+ 6

16

6
2
+ 1

8

10

3
7
+ 4

3
4
+ 1

6
6
+ 9

13

17

Write the numbers in each caterpillar in order from least to greatest.

55   57   56   59   58

1. ___ ___ ___ ___ ___

10   11   15   19   16

2. ___ ___ ___ ___ ___

70   43   69   82   67

3. ___ ___ ___ ___ ___

97   92   101   105   93

4. ___ ___ ___ ___ ___

Solve each problem. Use the key to color the picture.

4 = red   10 = blue   5 = green
12 = yellow   6 = orange

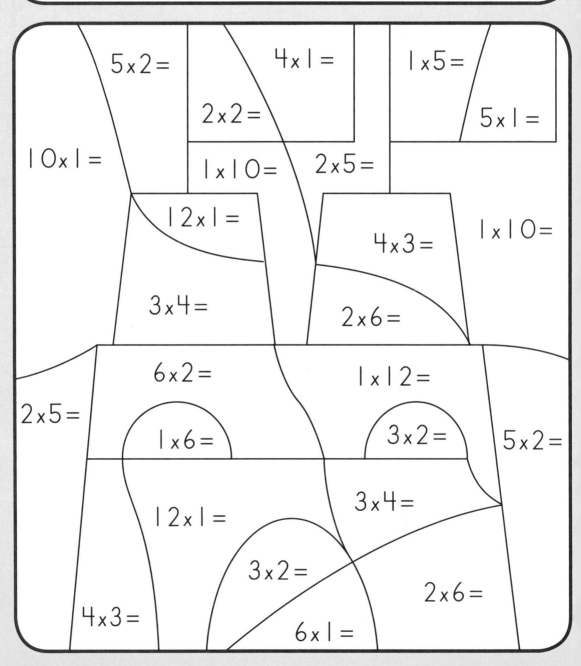

5 x 2 =

4 x 1 =

1 x 5 =

2 x 2 =

5 x 1 =

10 x 1 =

1 x 10 =

2 x 5 =

12 x 1 =

4 x 3 =

1 x 10 =

3 x 4 =

2 x 6 =

6 x 2 =

1 x 12 =

2 x 5 =

1 x 6 =

3 x 2 =

5 x 2 =

12 x 1 =

3 x 4 =

3 x 2 =

2 x 6 =

4 x 3 =

6 x 1 =

If a statement is true, circle the letter under **yes**. If a statement is false, circle the letter under **no**. To solve the riddle, write the circled letters in order on the lines.

		yes	no
1.	3 > 5	B	M
2.	2 < 1	R	U
3.	4 > 3	S	A
4.	8 < 6	N	H
5.	5 < 3	L	R
6.	9 > 7	O	T
7.	7 < 2	D	O
8.	1 < 4	M	E

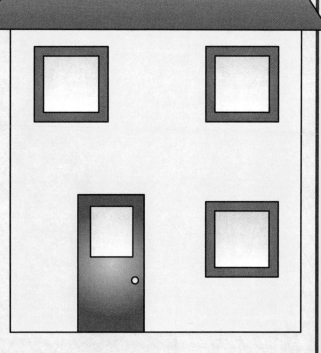

What room has no doors and no windows?

A _____ _____ _____ _____ _____ _____ _____ _____

Write the missing numbers to complete each pattern and help each rocket complete its countdown.

Rocket 1 (counting down by 1):
10
___
7
6
___
4
3
___
1

Rocket 2 (counting down by 5):
50
___
35
___
25
___
15
10

Rocket 3 (counting down by 2):
___
14
12
___
___
6
___
2

 CD-104367

The rocket lifted off on Friday, May 4, at 8:00 A.M. Use the chart to answer the questions and help the astronauts find their lift-off time in different parts of the world.

Kennedy Space Center	8:00 A.M.	Friday, May 4
Rome, Italy	2:00 P.M.	Friday, May 4
Tokyo, Japan	9:00 P.M.	Friday, May 4
Nairobi, Kenya	3:00 P.M.	Friday, May 4
Lima, Peru	7:00 A.M.	Friday, May 4
Sydney, Australia	10:00 P.M.	Friday, May 4
Vancouver, Canada	5:00 A.M.	Friday, May 4
Tel Aviv, Israel	3:00 P.M.	Friday, May 4
Moscow, Russia	4:00 P.M.	Friday, May 4

1. What time was it in Moscow? _____

2. Was it daytime or nighttime in Tokyo? _____

3. What is the time difference in hours between Lima and Vancouver? _____

4. How many hours earlier is it in Tel Aviv than in Sydney? _____

5. What is the time difference in hours between Nairobi and Kennedy Space Center? _____

6. Look at a clock to see what time it is. Which city has the time that is closest to your time right now? _____

Solve each problem. Match the answers to the numbers below. Write the correct letters on the lines.

24 +13 T	14 − 9 E	45 +27 W	20 −13 T
33 +29 P	96 −47 L	31 − 6 N	12 +75 D
21 −19 S	55 +36 H	65 −32 O	13 +44 A

What is as big as an elephant but weighs nothing at all?

,

__ __ __ __ __ __ __ __ __ __ __
57 25 5 49 5 62 91 57 25 7 2

__ __ __ __ __ __
2 91 57 87 33 72